This book belongs to:

_____

ISBN: 978-1-7343288-0-6
Library of Congress Control Number: 2019920746
Printed in the United States of America.

First printing, 2020.

Artist: Demitrius Motion Bullock
Compiler: Michelle Bullock

Spirited Moon Inspirations, LLC
175 Strafford Ave, Suite One
PMB# 309
Wayne, PA 19087

www.SpiritedMoonInspirations.com

Dedicated in loving remembrance of
"Gram"
Mary Rice

and to the inspiration of

James Shelton and T'ona Alazne'

I'm Like A BUTTERFLY

Written by
SPIRITED MOON

Illustrated by
Demitrius MOTION Bullock

I'm born in one image.
I'm born to transform.

I'm born yet again
to perform.

I'm like a butterfly.

It's true.

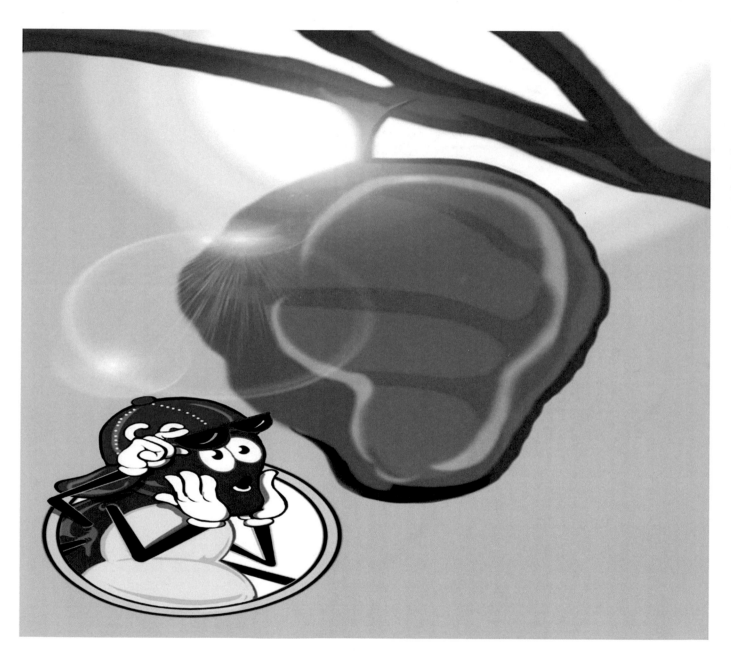

I'm like a butterfly.

So are you.

I'm learning and growing everyday.

I'm becoming more beautiful in every way.

I'm like a butterfly...
It's true.

I'm like a butterfly.
So are you.

I'm like a butterfly.

I spread my wings and fly.

I'm showing my true colors

as I grace the sky.

I'm showing the world

that I can fly high.

I'm like a butterfly.

It's true.

I'm like a butterfly

and so are you!

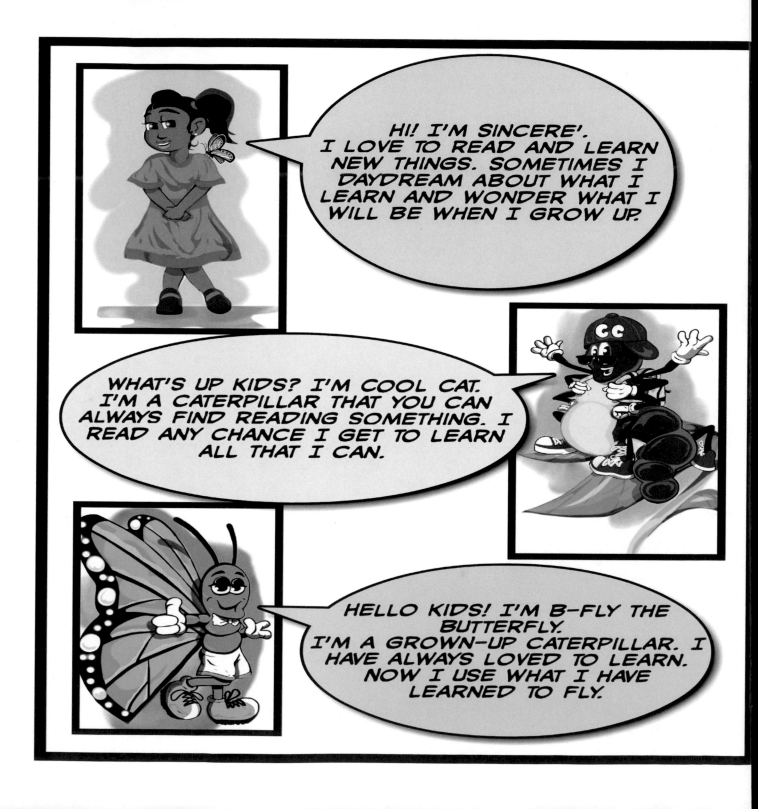

Spirited Moon

Just as the moon captures the ambiance of the Sun it is the aspiration of the author to reflect the light of Inspiration with positive intention and love. Spirited Moon is inspired to write poetic stories by her young daughter T'ona as well as from her own life experiences to address various challenges that face our youth. She writes to encourage everyone that they are special within their own uniqueness, valued and to live with purpose.

Demitrius "Motion" Bullock, artist and illustrator, has a portfolio of work that includes a number of logo creations and designs for a wide variety of industries. He has illustrated 22 publications to date which include book cover designs for a number of independent book authors, children's books and comic book illustrations. He is a self-taught artist from the Bronx, NY in multiple mediums. He was inspired by early street artists he witnessed as a child and his fascination with comic and graphic art led him to develop several of his own characters. He continues drawing and creating his own artwork and the building of his business Motion Illustrationz with his wife Michelle and son Bryce. Follow him on Instagram @ Demitrius_Motion_Bullock.

Made in the USA
Middletown, DE
07 June 2021